Visions and Ecstasies

David Zwirner Books

ekphrasis

Visions and Ecstasies
Selected Essays
H.D.

Contents

H.D. in Egypt, 1923

Old Forms, New Environments

Michael Green

Beyond life there is death, beyond exuberance, there is inevitable decay. Equally beyond death, there is life, old forms in new environments.
—H.D., "Curled Thyme"

The essays by the American writer H.D. (1886–1961) brought together in this new volume, many published here for the first time, present an imaginative landscape populated with the art and mythologies of ancient Greece. Best known for her poetry, H.D. was also a novelist, memoirist, essayist, and translator, though she frequently blended these forms as well. The texts collected here from her critical writings share with her wider literary project a concern with the art and poetry of the Hellenic world, as well as the mysteries of the creative process itself.

This interest in Greek poetry and art was also shared by Ezra Pound and Richard Aldington (whom H.D. would marry in 1913). Shortly following H.D.'s arrival in London in 1911, after a short stay in New York, the three poets established the avant-garde literary movement Imagism. Their new form of poetry favored precise, crystalline imagery achieved through reduced language and compressed expression. The stark evocations of the natural world in H.D.'s poetry collection *Sea Garden* (1916) exemplify this style. This group would later include other prominent writers—notably, Amy Lowell and D. H. Lawrence—who contributed to such groundbreaking publications as the literary magazine *The Egoist*, for which H.D. briefly served as an assistant editor. The essays in this volume show a different, though not wholly disconnected, side to H.D.'s oeuvre than the Imagist poetry that has established her work within the canon of literary modernism.

In 1918, in an effort to escape the turbulent fallout from World War I in London, H.D. relocated to a house aptly named Peace Cottage, in rural Buckinghamshire. Like many on the home front, H.D. experienced a series of cataclysms: her brother, Gilbert, was killed in action, and her father, Charles, grieving the death of his son, died soon after. In March 1919, H.D. found herself stricken with double pneumonia at Saint Faith's Nursing Home, Ealing, while nine months pregnant with her second child (her first was stillborn in 1915). She was forewarned that she and the baby would likely not survive the birth. Her already fraught marriage to Aldington, who had just returned from serving on the front line in France, continued to falter as Aldington exhibited symptoms of post-traumatic stress disorder, and H.D. suffered numerous psychological breakdowns as these devastating events converged.

On March 31, 1919, H.D.'s daughter, Frances Perdita Aldington, was born, and both mother and child survived. In July, H.D.'s new companion, Bryher, took her to Cornwall's untamed Scilly Isles, which served as a rehabilitative return to nature, friendship, and writing. Bryher, born Annie Winifred Ellerman, first met H.D. a year before this trip and cared for her while at Saint Faith's. Their important union no doubt aided H.D.'s recovery following her harrowing experiences.

"Notes on Thought and Vision," the first text in this volume, is the result of their journey to the Scilly Isles. Merging prose and poetry and serving as a critique of art and literature, as well as a philosophy of H.D.'s own artistic project, it is one of the author's few completed meditations on aesthetics and the creative process. The essay opens with a staccato mantra: "Three states or manifestations of life: body, mind, over-mind." Then: "Aim of men and women of highest development is equilibrium, balance, growth of the three at once." These three states—physical, mental, and spiritual, maybe even divine—entwine to generate a balance necessary for reaching what H.D. considers the highest development, "over-mind consciousness." Anyone can cultivate over-mind, so long as he or she stimulates the manifestations of life: the body must feel desire and be open to pleasure, the mind must search with intellect, and the body and mind must be in balance to achieve an over-mind that is normal and sane.

H.D. conjures her own experience of this over-mind state as an aqueous cap that covers her head, blurring her vision. She describes the cap as "transparent, fluid yet with definite body . . . like a closed sea-plant, jelly-fish or anemone." (Moon jelly, or *Aurelia aurita*, stalk the surface of the Scilly Isles' waters, their luminous bells swollen and their medusa-like tentacles swaying.) This "jelly-fish experience" symbolizes a higher state of consciousness that affords a new type of vision and focus, a clarity that transforms artistic expression and, specifically for H.D., one's relationship with art. As mystifying as it may seem, this transcendent, ecstatic condition was decidedly experiential for H.D.

As the tendrils of the jellyfish, the "super-feelers," stretch down through her body, they center in her "love-region," a space of consciousness that she terms "womb-vision." The visions of the brain and womb come together in ecstasy to form over-mind consciousness. In this context, H.D. asks, "Is it easier for a woman to attain this state of consciousness than for a man?" She answers by noting that she first recognized the jellyfish cap when she was pregnant with her daughter. Understanding and experiencing the body is the first step toward joining the visions of brain and womb, and here H.D. allows women an intellectual and bodily agency that was previously denied by the misogyny of many of her contemporaries.

H.D. then guides us to the ancient Eleusinian Mysteries, sacred rites that were performed annually at Eleusis to celebrate the reunion of the goddess Demeter and her abducted daughter, Persephone. A look at the myth invoked in this reference brings greater clarity to H.D.'s privileging of the female body. The myth tells of a separation and then a union restored: Zeus abducts Persephone from her mother, goddess of agriculture, and bequeaths her to Hades, king of the underworld. As Demeter mourns her loss, crops die, lands freeze, and harvests no longer bear fruit. Under duress from the cries of starving mortals, Zeus orders Persephone's return to the world of the living. This reunion brings life and fertility back to the earth. We might then read H.D.'s companionship with Bryher and the birth of her daughter as the foundation for a new creativity, or, rather, a creative vision realized in relation to the female body and established in a time of (re)union. The energy of the womb and childbirth gives rise to artistic energy.[1] Crucially, for H.D., without these female relationships and without intimacy, the body's desires remain unmoved and thus over-mind consciousness becomes unattainable. But once attained, the state of over-mind consciousness enables H.D. to revisit past worlds and discover windows into the over-mind of others.[2]

The four essays following "Notes on Thought and Vision" draw us to the Hellenic poets Anacreon and Theocritus, and to the travel writings of Pausanias.[3] In "From Megara to Corinth," Athens becomes something of a refuge for H.D., away from the terrors of war, and statues lining the Acropolis appeal "to the intellect." We find a similar opposition to the battlefield in "People of Sparta," where H.D. reflects on how the scene of war exists beyond technical, artistic expression. In "A Poet in the Wilderness," she describes reading Anacreon's poems through touch. This attentive, meditative action physically connects H.D. to the poet's verses, and returning to "Notes on Thought and Vision," we can see this as "sympathy of thought" in action.

As readers, we might take the notion of "sympathy of thought"—a sharing of intellect and ideas that acknowledges one's subjectivity and creative potential, and a foundational step toward achieving over-mind—as our cue to enter the animated vista of myths, places, and characters that H.D. lays before us. Indeed, as H.D. writes, "The realization of this over-conscious world is the concern of the artist. But this world is there for everyone."

1   Donna Krolik Hollenberg reaches a similar conclusion when she writes that in "Notes on Thought and Vision," H.D. "first attempts to articulate a theory of creativity based on the emotional issues arising from her trauma in childbirth." See Donna Krolik Hollenberg, *H.D.: The Poetics of Childbirth and Creativity* (Boston: Northeastern University Press, 1991), p. 19.

2   H.D.'s relationship with the ancient past is lucidly interpreted by Henry Rushton Fairclough in his 1926 address to the American Philological Association, in which he announced that H.D. "has completely transported herself into the Hellenic past, or, shall we say, that she has made ancient Hellas live again in the present." Fairclough's speech was later published as *The Classics and Our Twentieth-Century Poets* (Stanford: Stanford University Press, 1927).

3   The four essays are extracted from the typewritten manuscript of *Notes on Euripides, Pausanias, and Greek Lyric Poets*. This compendium of fourteen critical writings lays out what many scholars have come to characterize as H.D.'s alternative survey of Greek art, poetry, and thought. Dating these essays has been the subject of much discussion and debate, as they were composed independently of one another and later brought together. "People of Sparta" was published in the monthly literary magazine *Bookman* in December 1924. For one of the most detailed accounts of this manuscript and more on their dating, see Eileen Gregory, *H.D. and Hellenism: Classic Lines* (Cambridge: Cambridge University Press, 1997). Gregory indicates that H.D. most likely started writing the four essays included in this volume in the fall of 1920, while staying with Bryher in California. In this edition, we have striven to respect H.D.'s original texts as much as possible by maintaining and standardizing British spelling, syntax, and conventions. We have applied this style to "Notes on Thought and Vision," previously published by City Lights Books, for greater readability and consistency. In certain rare cases, we have made slight modifications to grammar and punctuation to reflect contemporary usage.

Notes on Thought and Vision

Scilly Islands
July 1919

Three states or manifestations of life: body, mind, over-mind.

Aim of men and women of highest development is equilibrium, balance, growth of the three at once; brain without physical strength is a manifestation of weakness, a disease comparable to cancerous growth or tumour; body without reasonable amount of intellect is an empty fibrous bundle of glands as ugly and little to be desired as body of a victim of some form of elephantiasis or fatty-degeneracy; over-mind without the balance of the other two is madness and a person so developed should have as much respect as a reasonable maniac and no more.

~

All reasoning, normal, sane and balanced men and women need and seek at certain times of their lives, certain definite physical relationships. Men and women of temperament, musicians, scientists, artists especially, need these relationships to develop and draw forth their talents. Not to desire and make every effort to develop along these natural physical lines, cripples and dwarfs the being. To shun, deny and belittle such experiences is to bury one's talent carefully in a napkin.

~

When a creative scientist, artist or philosopher has been for some hours or days intent on his work, his mind often takes on an almost physical character. That is, his mind becomes his real body. His over-mind becomes his brain.

When Leonardo da Vinci worked, his brain was Leonardo, the personality, Leonardo da Vinci. He saw the faces of many of his youths and babies and young women definitely with his over-mind. The *Madonna of the Rocks* is not a picture. It is a window. We look through a window into the world of pure over-mind.

~

If I could visualize or describe that over-mind in my own case, I should say this: it seems to me that a cap is over my head, a cap of consciousness over my head, my forehead, affecting a little my eyes. Sometimes when I am in that state of consciousness, things about me appear slightly blurred as if seen under water.

Ordinary things never become quite unreal nor disproportionate. It is only an effort to readjust, to focus, seemingly a slight physical effort.

~

That over-mind seems a cap, like water, transparent, fluid yet with definite body, contained in a definite space. It is like a closed sea-plant, jelly-fish or anemone.

Into that over-mind, thoughts pass and are visible like fish swimming under clear water.

~

The swing from normal consciousness to abnormal consciousness is accompanied by grinding discomfort of mental agony.

~

I should say—to continue this jelly-fish metaphor—that long feelers reached down and through the body, that these stood in the same relation to the nervous system as the over-mind to the brain or intellect.

There is, then, a set of super-feelings. These feelings extend out and about us; as the long, floating tentacles of the jelly-fish reach out and about him. They are not of different material, extraneous, as the physical arms and legs are extraneous to the grey matter of the direct-ing brain. The super-feelers are part of the super-mind, as the jelly-fish feelers are the jelly-fish itself, elongated in fine threads.

I first realized this state of consciousness in my head. I visualize it just as well, now, centred in the love-region of the body or placed like a foetus in the body.

The centre of consciousness is either the brain or the love-region of the body.

~

Is it easier for a woman to attain this state of conscious-ness than for a man?

For me, it was before the birth of my child that the jelly-fish consciousness seemed to come definitely into the field or realm of the intellect or brain.

~

Are these jelly-fish states of consciousness interchange-able? Should we be able to think with the womb and feel with the brain?

May this consciousness be centred entirely in the brain or entirely in the womb or corresponding love-region of a man's body?

~

Vision is of two kinds—vision of the womb and vision of the brain. In vision of the brain, the region of consciousness is above and about the head; when the centre of consciousness shifts and the jelly-fish is in the body (I visualize it in my case lying on the left side with the streamers or feelers floating up toward the brain), we have vision of the womb or love-vision.

~

The majority of dream and of ordinary vision is vision of the womb.

The brain and the womb are both centres of consciousness, equally important.

~

Most of the so-called artists of today have lost the use of their brain. There is no way of arriving at the over-mind, except through the intellect. To arrive at the world of over-mind vision any other way is to be the thief that climbs into the sheep-fold.

I believe there are artists coming in the next generation, some of whom will have the secret of using their over-minds.

~

Over-mind artists usually come in a group. There were the great Italians: Verrocchio, Angelo, Ghiberti, the lot that preceded and followed da Vinci, including statesmen, explorers, and men and women of curious and sensitive development.

There was the great Athenian group: the dramatists, Socrates, the craftsmen and the men and women, their followers and lovers.

~

There is no great art period without great lovers.

~

Socrates' whole doctrine of vision was a doctrine of love.

We must be "in love" before we can understand the mysteries of vision.

A lover must choose one of the same type of mind as himself, a musician, a musician, a scientist, a scientist, a general, a young man also interested in the theory and practice of arms and armies.

We begin with sympathy of thought.

The minds of the two lovers merge, interact in sympathy of thought.

The brain, inflamed and excited by this interchange of ideas, takes on its character of over-mind, becomes (as I have visualized in my own case) a jelly-fish, placed over and about the brain.

The love-region is excited by the appearance or beauty of the loved one, its energy not dissipated in physical relation, takes on its character of mind, becomes this womb-brain or love-brain that I have visualized as a jelly-fish *in* the body.

The love-brain and over-brain are both capable of thought. This thought is vision.

~

All men have possibilities of developing this vision.

The over-mind is like a lens of an opera-glass. When we are able to use this over-mind lens, the whole world of vision is open to us.

I have said that the over-mind is a lens. I should say more exactly that the love-mind and the over-mind are two lenses. When these lenses are properly adjusted, focused, they bring the world of vision into consciousness. The two work separately, perceive separately, yet make one picture.

~

The mystic, the philosopher is content to contemplate, to examine these pictures. The Attic dramatist reproduced them for men of lesser or other gifts. He realized, the whole time, that they were not his ideas. They were eternal, changeless ideas that he had grown aware of, dramas already conceived that he had watched; memory is the mother, begetter of all drama, idea, music, science or song.

~

We may enter the world of over-mind consciousness directly, through the use of our over-mind brain. We may enter it indirectly, in various ways. Every person must work out his own way.

Certain words and lines of Attic choruses, any scrap of da Vinci's drawings, the Delphic charioteer, have a definite, hypnotic effect on me. They are straight, clear entrances, to me, to over-world consciousness. But my line of approach, my sign-posts, are not your sign-posts.

~

My sign-posts are not yours, but if I blaze my own trail, it may help to give you confidence and urge you to get out of the murky, dead, old, thousand-times explored old world, the dead world of overworked emotions and thoughts.

But the world of the great creative artists is never dead.

The new schools of destructive art theorists are on the wrong track. Because Leonardo and his kind are never old, never dead. Their world is never explored, hardly even entered. Because it needs an over-mind or a slight glimmering of over-mind intelligence to understand over-mind intelligence.

~

The Delphic charioteer has, I have said, an almost hypnotic effect on me: the bend of his arm, the knife-cut of his chin; his feet, rather flat, slightly separated, a firm pedestal for himself; the fall of his drapery, in geometrical precision; and the angles of the ingatherings of the drapery at the waist.

All this was no "inspiration", it was sheer, hard brain work.

This figure has been created by a formula arrived at consciously or unconsciously.

If we had the right sort of brains, we would receive a definite message from that figure, like dots and lines ticked off by one receiving station, received and translated into definite thought by another telegraphic centre.

There is no trouble about art. There is already enough beauty in the world of art, enough in the fragments and the almost perfectly preserved charioteer at Delphi alone to remake the world.

There is no trouble about art, it is the appreciators we want. We want young men and women to communicate with the charioteer and his like.

We want receiving centres for dots and dashes.

~

It is said that da Vinci went mad if he saw a boy's face in Florence or a caged bird or a child with yellow hair that fell or stood up in tight whorls like the goldsmith work he had learned with Verrocchio. Da Vinci went mad because those lines of the bird's back or the boy's shoulder or the child's hair acted on him directly, as the lines of a statue, worked out like the charioteer, would act on us if we had the right sort of receiving brain.

~

Two or three people, with healthy bodies and the right sort of receiving brains, could turn the whole tide of human thought, could direct lightning flashes of electric power to slash across and destroy the world of dead, murky thought.

Two or three people gathered together in the name of truth, beauty, over-mind consciousness could bring the whole force of this power back into the world.

~

It is true that, in the year A.D. 361, the Galilean conquered at Delphi. That was because the Hellenic mind had entirely lost the secret of dots and dashes. The electric force of the lines and angles of the priest-like body of the charioteer still gave out their message but there was no one to receive this message.

The Galilean conquered because he was a great artist, like da Vinci.

A fish-basket, upturned on the sand, or a candle in a candle-stick or a Roman coin with its not unbeautifully wrought head of a king, could excite him and give him ideas, as the bird or boy's face or child's yellow hair gave da Vinci ideas.

~

The Galilean fell in love with things as well as people. He would fall in love with a sea-gull or some lake-heron that would dart up from the coarse lake grass, when Peter leapt out to drag his great boat on shore, or the plain little speckled-backed birds bought in the market by the poor Jews. Then, he would look at Peter with his great archaic head and the young Jude with his intense eyes, and he would exclaim suddenly: "Ah, but your faces, your faces are more beautiful, more charged with ideas, with lines that suggest and bring me into touch with the world of over-mind thought, than many, many sparrows."

~

He looked at the blue grass-lily and the red-brown sand-lily that grew under the sheltered hot sand-banks in the southern winter, for hours and hours. If he closed his eyes, he saw every vein and fleck of blue or vermilion. He would breathe in the fragrance with the wind and the salt. He would rest for days along the shores of the sea-lakes.

Then, in the town, there would be some tragedy and he would send the friends and wailing relatives out of the way. He would be angry, as he looked at the little girl's face, that she was surrounded by such ugliness. He would look at her for a long time because of the beauty of the little, straight nose and the eyelids, the hair clinging like seaweed to the fine little skull, the very white hands. He would like to have stayed looking at her for hours, like the blue grass-lily. But he was afraid they would break in, suddenly again, with their heavy, black clothes, and ugly voices. So he said, "Daughter, I say unto you, arise."

~

The first step in the Eleusinian mysteries had to do with sex. There were images set up in a great room, coloured marbles and brown pottery, painted with red and vermilion and coloured earthen work or clay images. The candidates for admission to the mysteries would be shown through the room by a priest or would walk through at random, as the crowd walks through the pornographic chamber at the museum at Naples.

It would be easy enough to judge them by their attitude, whether it was one of crude animal enjoyment or hypocritical aloofness.

The crowd that got through to the second room would be different, more sensitive, more fastidious. They would correspond to certain of our intellectual types of today. They would be interested because it was the thing to be interested—also to show their superiority.

Any one who got safely through the mere animal stage and the intellectual stage would be left in a small room by himself to make his constatation.

~

Anyone who wants can get through these stages today just as easily as the Eleusinian candidates outside Athens in the fifth century B.C.

There is plenty of pornographic literature that is interesting and amusing.

If you cannot be entertained and instructed by Boccaccio, Rabelais, Montaigne, Sterne, Middleton, de Gourmont and de Régnier there is something wrong with you physically.

If you cannot read these people and enjoy them you are not ready for the first stage of initiation.

~

If you do read these people and enjoy them and enjoy them really with your body, because you have a normal healthy body, then you may be ready for the second stage of initiation.

You can look into things with your intellect, with your sheer brain.

~

If your brain cannot stand the strain of following out these lines of thought, scientifically, and if you are not balanced and sane enough to grasp these things with a certain amount of detachment, you are obviously not ready for experiments in over-mind consciousness.

~

Socrates said, "There are many wand-bearers but few inspired." He meant, by wand-bearers, people who had passed the first two stages of the Eleusinian mysteries. We mean by wand-bearers today, intelligent people of normal development, who have looked into matters of life scientifically and with a certain amount of artistic appreciation.

Today there are many wand-bearers but few inspired.

~

One must understand a lower wisdom before one understands a higher. One must understand Euripides before one understands Aristophanes. Yet to understand dung chemically and spiritually and with the earth sense, one must first understand the texture, spiritual and chemical and earthy, of the rose that grows from it.

Euripides is a white rose, lyric, feminine, a spirit. Aristophanes is a satyr.

Is the satyr greater or less than the white rose it embraces? Is the earth greater or less than the white rose it brings forth? Is the dung greater or less than the rose?

~

Flowers are made to seduce the senses: fragrance, form, colour.

If you cannot be seduced by beauty, you cannot learn the wisdom of ugliness.

~

Zeus Endendros—God in a tree; Dionysus Anthios, God in a flower; Zeus Melios, God in the black earth, death, disruption, disintegration; Dionysus Zagreus, the flower torn, broken by chemical process of death, vein, leaf, texture—white luminous lily surface, veined with black—white lily flesh bruised, withered. "I, Lais, place my mirror here at thy feet, O Paphian—I remember and I dare not remember. Is there a mystery beyond that of thy white arms, O Aphrogenia? Is there a beauty greater than the white pear-branch which broke so white against a black April storm sky that Zeus himself was roused from his sacred meditation, as from the ranges of Olympos he gazed below upon the Attic pastures. He gazed below and saw you, O white branch. He was angry, for you were more white against the sky than the passion of his shaft. For that reason he sent lightning to blast you, O tree. Since then no man may speak your name, O Goddess. But we know there is a mystery greater than beauty and that is death."

~

The heat, the stench of things, the unutterable boredom of it all, Meleager of Gadara, what a fate; a Jew father, a Greek mother. What God of the Hebrew, what daemon of the islands had presided at his ill-omened begetting? Heliodora, Zenophile, what were they but names? Greek prostitutes—branded by Syrian traders and Jew merchants alike. The stench—the dust, Meleager of Gadara—what a fate.

No wind and the sea stretching like the dead parchment rent with the devil tokens—the Hebrew script he would die to forget—the tongue he would die to forget—but that in dying he would forget that other—gold—light of gold—words, potent, a charm each leading to a world where there were cold flowers.

Heliodora, Zenophile—no Attic hetairas.

Flowers?

The roses that he had touched that morning—the boy at the wharf pier—he had stepped from a boat, wet with the sea about the islands. But the boy's wet curls smelt of salt fish and his roses were already rank—rotting—

and he had dipped their streaked stems in cheap myrrh to cheat the Heliodoras of this world of their sparse [...]

Gods, dead alike of Greek and Hebrew. What devil had sent a swine, a pig to plant its two feet on his door step and gaze within? Voices and shouting. He would never find peace that day for the golden branch of the divine Plate ever shining by its own light.

A pig on the door step.

To live with a poet's mind in a slum of Gadara. Meleager—what daemon of the islands was present at your ill-omened begetting?

To live with a poet's mind in a slum of Gadara or to live with princely Jews his father's friend—a merchant respected—his father again—in the palaces of Syrian princes.

There was no choice—*but a pig on the door step*.

Avaunt pig! Must I sacrifice the script of the golden Plate to hurl at that pig?

After all, could the script of the golden highfalutin high-sounding Plate be put to a better use?

He ignores the script, save to turn it over with his snout. What devil possesses him?

Well, here is my Gadarene foot then.

A herd of them in the street.

Beyond the stifling dust, someone is shouting. A voice, more portent than the script of the golden Plate. Speaking Greek too.

"Be you entered into the sea."

Praise every god of Greek or Hebrew they are gone.

A crowd of the usual slum vandals—and one young man who is laughing.

~

A princely stranger and his father, a Jew too. What cool hands at parting.

Beyond the Zenophiles of this world there is another Zenophile, beyond the Heliodoras another Heliodora, beyond the dank, hot and withering roses, other roses.

A princely stranger and a poet.

I would make him some gift, for his brow was more lordly (though his father was no Greek) than the Kyllenian Hermes.

I would bind narcissus to narcissus. I would plait the red violet to the white violet. I would break for you one rose, more red than the wine-cyclamen. I would bind the stem of the crocus to the stem of the wild hyacinth, that each might show less lovely about your brow, Kyllenian Hermes.

~

Egypt in the terms of world-consciousness is the act of love. Hellas is a child born.

The secret of the Sphinx is the secret of knowledge. The secret of the Centaur is the secret of feeling.

The Sphinx knows everything. The Centaur feels everything.

~

Three worlds.

1. World of abstraction: Helios, Athene.
2. Intermediate or Nature world: Pan, the Naiads.

3. World of the uninitiate men and women.

All these worlds are important, equally important. But we are important only insofar as we become identified with the highest in ourselves—"our own familiar daemon".

~

Spirits of a higher world have access into a lower world. Athene may appear to one in the next lower world. She may be the companion of a half-god, but she must preserve her dignity, her Olympian character. Athene perfectly did this. Therefore the gods accepted and enrolled Odysseus among the half-gods and heroes.

But when there was a question of Artemis losing caste by her association with the too boorish giant, Orion, the giant was slain.

However, lest honour should be lacking the Olympian hierarchy because of this lapse of taste, Orion was afterward received among the stars.

~

It was *de rigueur* for an Olympian not to appear to a mortal direct. Therefore Selene who requested this was burned to ash.

But we have many records of Naiads, tree and river spirits, sea spirits and voices of the sea, and Centaurs holding friendly intercourse with mortals.

We also know that Pan appeared to those in pain or trouble, not only in dreams but "visibly at mid-day".

Pan appeared at Marathon before all the Greeks. And I know of witnesses today who have had vision of this god.

~

Normal consciousness, pricks of everyday discomfort, jealousy and despair and various forms of unhappiness that are the invariable accompaniment of any true, deep relationship, all this may be symbolized by a thistle.

There are two ways of escaping the pain and despair of life, and of the rarest, most subtle, dangerous and ensnaring gift that life can bring us, relationship with another person—love.

One way is to kill that love in one's heart. To kill love—to kill life.

The other way is to accept that love, to accept the snare, to accept the pricks, the thistle.

To accept life—but that is dangerous.

It is also dangerous not to accept life.

To every man and woman in the world it is given at some time or another, in some form or another, to make the choice.

Every man and woman is free to accept or deny life—to accept or reject this questionable gift—this thistle.

~

But these notes are concerned chiefly with the mental process that is in some form or other the complement of the life process.

That is to say this thistle—life, love, martyrdom—leads in the end—must lead in the logical course of events to death, paradise, peace.

That world of death—that is, death to the stings of life, which is the highest life—may be symbolized by the serpent.

The world of vision has been symbolized in all ages by various priestly cults in all countries by the serpent.

In my personal language or vision, I call this serpent a jelly-fish.

~

The serpent—the jelly-fish—the over-conscious mind.

The realization of this over-conscious world is the concern of the artist.

But this world is there for everyone.

The minds of men differ but the over-minds are alike.

~

Our minds, all of our minds, are like dull little houses, built more or less alike—a dull little city with rows of little detached villas, and here and there a more pretentious house, set apart from the rest, but in essentials, seen from a distance, one with the rest, all drab, all grey.

Each comfortable little home shelters a comfortable little soul—and a wall at the back shuts out completely any communication with the world beyond.

Man's chief concern is keeping his little house warm and making his little wall strong.

~

Outside is a great vineyard and grapes and rioting and madness and dangers.

It is very dangerous.

An enormous moth detached himself from a bunch of yellow grapes—he seemed stupefied with the heat of the sun—heavy with the sun and his soft belly swollen with the honey of the grapes, I would have said, for there was a bead of gold—resinous—that matted the feathers at his throat.

He fell rather than flew and his great feet scratched with a faint metallic ring the side of my golden cup.

He stumbled, awkward and righted himself, clutched the rim of my cup, waved his antennae feebly.

I would have rescued him but I myself was dizzy with the heat and the fumes of the golden wine and I heard a great shout of laughter as I tried to steady my cup and I shouted in reply, *he* is drunk—*he* is drunk.

So he was drunk.

Outside is a great vineyard and rioting and madness and dangers.

~

The body—limbs of a tree, branches of a fruit-tree, the whole body a tree—philosophy of the Tao, philosophy of the Hebrew, philosophy of the Greek, man identified with nature, the just man "a tree planted by the rivers", numerous instances of gods in trees and human beings of peculiar beauty or grace turned at death, as reward of kindliness, into trees, poplar trees, mulberry trees, laurels.

But a man has intellect, brain—a mind in fact, capable of three states of being, a mind that may be conscious in the ordinary, scholarly, literal sense of the word, or sub-conscious—those sub-conscious states varying in different states of dream or physical feeling, or illness, delirium or madness—a mind, over-conscious as well, able to enter into a whole life as Leonardo entered,

Euripides, the Galilean with his baskets and men's faces and Roman coins—the forest hermits of the Ganges and the painter who concentrated on one tuft of pine branch with its brown cone until every needle was a separate entity to him and every pine needle bore to every other one, a clear relationship like a drawing of a later mechanical twentieth-century bridge-builder.

~

Lo-fu sat in his orchard in the Ming dynasty, A.D. 184. He sat in his orchard and looked about in a vague, casual way. Against the grey stones of the orchard wall he saw the low branch of an apple tree. He thought, That shoot should have been pruned, it hangs too low. Then as he looked at the straight tough young shoot, he thought, No, the apples are excellent, so round and firm. Then he went on looking.

It was a shoot of some years' growth. Why had it been left untrimmed? Was it some special experiment in grafting the old gardener had undertaken some years ago? Was it by accident that the limb hung there? Then his conscious mind ceased wondering and, being an artist, his intensity and concentration were of a special order and he looked at that fruit branch hanging in the sun, the globes of the apples red, yellow, red with flecks of brown and red, yellow where the two colours merged, and flecks of brown again on the yellow, and green as the round surface curved in toward the stem. He saw the stem, pushed down almost lost in the green hollow. He saw the stem fastened to the tough little branch above.

He saw the green brown bark of the stem and he compared it with the darker, stronger bark of the branch. He examined the ridges and the minute black lines that made up the individual surface of that little branch. He went further. There were two leaves, continents to be explored in a leisurely manner lest his mind passing one carelessly from vein to vein, should miss one rib or the small branch of one off-shoot of that exquisite skeleton. And when he knew the skeleton of that leaf, the rivers, as it were, furrowing that continent, his mind was content. But it had only begun its search. Between each river there lay a fair green field—many, many little fields each with an individuality, each with some definite feature setting it apart from every other little plot.

~

I have tried to tell in a small way with as little detail as possible how Lo-fu looked at that branch. He really did look at it. He really did see it. Then he went inside and in his little cool room out of the sun he closed his eyes. He saw that branch but more clearly, more vividly than ever. That branch was his mistress now, his love. As he saw it in the orchard, that mistress was, as it were, observed in a crowd, from a distance. He could not touch her, his mistress with all the world about. Here, in his little room, the world had ceased to exist. It was shut off, shut out, forgotten. His love, his apple branch, his beautiful subtle mistress, was his. And having possessed her with his great and famished soul, she was his forever.

~

She was his, and though he knew she was only one, one of a thousand women, one of a thousand, thousand, beautiful women, she was his, his own. And he was never jealous, though her beauty was so obvious, for no one else could possess her. Yet unlike another lover, he longed that his friend should love her too, or should make another branch his own, for the orchard was full and beyond the orchard the mountain and pine forests were a thousand intimate friendly herbs and grasses.

Lo-fu was a poet. To him that apple branch, outside in the orchard, existed as an approach to something else. As the body of a man's mistress might be said to exist as the means of approach to something else, that is as a means or instrument of feeling or happiness, so the branch in the orchard existed to Lo-fu as the means of attaining happiness, as a means of completing himself, as a means of approach to ecstasy.

~

I have been talking with a young man, a scholar and philosopher. He says my term over-mind is not good, because in his case at least, the mental state I describe lies below the sub-conscious mind. That is, I visualize my three states of consciousness in a row,

1. Over-conscious mind.
2. Conscious mind.
3. Sub-conscious mind.

He on the other hand visualizes his three states,

1. Conscious mind.
2. Sub-conscious mind.

3. Universal mind.

He means by universal mind exactly what I mean by over-mind but certainly my term over-mind is not adequate, if this over-mind state is approached by others through the sub-conscious.

But we both visualize these states in a row, though I suppose the universal symbol is the triangle, or taken a step further, the circle, as the three seem to run into one another, though neither he nor I visualize them that way.

~

The body of a man is a means of approach, or can be used as a means of approach to ecstasy. Man's body can be used for that. The best Greek sculpture used the bodies of young athletes as Lo-fu used the branch of the fruit tree. The lines of the human body may be used as an approach to the over-mind or universal mind.

The lines of the human body and the lines of the fruit tree are like the body of the Delphic charioteer that I spoke of some time ago. The fruit tree and the human body are both receiving stations, capable of storing up energy, over-world energy. That energy is always there but can be transmitted only to another body or another mind that is in sympathy with it, or keyed to the same pitch.

The body of the Greek boy Polycleitus used for his Diadumenos was as impersonal a thing as a tree. He used the body instead of a tree. That boy's body was, of course, capable of human passions but Polycleitus' approach to that body was not through the human passions.

But of course he was in love with it just as Lo-fu was in love with apple branch and Leonardo with the boy's face or the Galilean with the field lilies.

~

But the body, I suppose, like a lump of coal, fulfils its highest function when it is being consumed.

When coal burns it gives off heat.

The body consumed with love gives off heat.

But taken a step further, coal may be used to make gas, an essence, a concentrated ethereal form of coal.

So with the body. It may burn out simply as heat or physical love. That may be good. But it is also interesting to understand the process whereby the heat of the physical body is transmuted to this other, this different form, concentrated, ethereal, which we refer to in common speech as spirit.

It is all spirit but spirit in different forms.

We cannot have the heat without the lump of coal.

Perhaps so we cannot have spirit without body, the body of nature, or the body of individual men and women.

~

I spoke to a scientist, a psychologist, about my divisions of mind and over-mind. He said that over-mind was not exactly the right term, that sub-conscious mind was the phrase I was groping for.

I have thought for a long time about the comparative value of these terms, and I see at last my fault and his.

We were both wrong. I was about to cover too much

of the field of abnormal consciousness by the term over-mind. He, on the other hand, would have called it all sub-conscious mind.

But the sub-conscious and the over-conscious are entirely different states, entirely different worlds.

~

The sub-conscious world is the world of sleeping dreams and the world great lovers enter, physical lovers, but very great ones.

The over-conscious world is the world of waking dreams and the world great lovers enter, spiritual lovers, but only the greatest.

~

A sub-conscious dream may become an over-conscious dream at the moment of waking.

~

The intellect, the brain, the conscious mind is the bridge across, the link between the sub-conscious and the over-conscious.

I think at last I have my terms clear.

There are three states of manifestations—sub-conscious mind, conscious mind, over-conscious mind.

~

These jelly-fish, I think, are the "seeds cast into the ground". But as it takes a man and woman to create another life, so it takes these two forms of seed, one in the head and one in the body, to make a new spiritual birth. I think that is why I saw them as jelly-fish. They are really two flecks of protoplasm and when we are "born again", we begin not as a child but as the very first germs that grow into a child.

~

Probably we pass through all forms of life and that is very interesting. But so far I have passed through these two, I am in my spiritual body a jelly-fish and a pearl.

We can probably use this pearl, as a crystal ball is used, for concentrating and directing pictures from the world of vision.

~

It is necessary to work, to strive toward the understanding of the over-mind. But once a man becomes conscious of this jelly-fish above his head, this pearl within his skull, this seed cast into the ground, his chief concern automatically becomes his body.

Once we become concretely aware of this pearl, this seed, our centre of consciousness shifts. Our concern is with the body.

~

Where does the body come in?

What is the body?

~

I imagine it has often been said that the body is like an oyster and the soul or spirit, a pearl. But today I saw for myself that the jelly-fish over my head had become concentrated. I saw that the state of mind I had before symbolized as a jelly-fish was just as well symbolized differently. That is, all the spiritual energy seemed concentrated in the middle of my forehead, inside my skull, and it was small and giving out a very soft light, but not scattered light, light concentrated in itself as the light of a pearl would be. So I understood exactly what the Galilean meant by the kingdom of heaven, being a pearl of great price.

Then in the same relation, the body was not a very rare or lovely thing. The body seemed an elementary, unbeautiful and transitory form of life. Yet here again, I saw that the body had its use. The oyster makes the pearl in fact. So the body, with all its emotions and fears and pain in time casts off the sprit, a concentrated essence, not itself, but made, in a sense, created by itself.

I know that this has been said before but I speak for myself, from my personal experience.

Because the spirit, we realize, is a seed. No man by thought can add an inch to his stature, no initiate by the strength and power of his intellect can force his spirit to grow.

He cannot force his spirit to grow, but he can retard its growth. At least so it seems to me.

He can retard its growth by neglect of his body because the body of man as the body of nature is the ground into which the seed or spirit is cast.

This is the mystery of Demeter, the Earth Mother. The body of the Eleusinian initiate had become one with the earth, as his soul had become one with the seeds enclosed in the earth.

No man by thought can make the grain sprout or the acorn break its shell. No man by intellectual striving can make his spirit expand.

But every man can till the field, can clear weeds from about the stems of flowers.

Every man can water his own little plot, can strive to quiet down the overwrought tension of his body.

~

Christ and his father, or as the Eleusinian mystic would have said, his mother, were one.

Christ was the grapes that hung against the sun-lit walls of that mountain garden, Nazareth. He was the white hyacinth of Sparta and the narcissus of the islands. He was the conch shell and the purple-fish left by the lake tides. He was the body of nature, the vine, the Dionysus, as he was the soul of nature.

He was the gulls screaming at low tide and tearing the small crabs from among the knotted weeds.

~

Christ and his father, or as the Eleusinian mystic would have said, his mother, were one.

Christ was the grapes that hung against the sun-lit walls of that mountain garden, Nazareth. He was the white hyacinth of Sparta and the narcissus of the islands. He was the conch shell and the purple-fish left by the lake tides. He was the body of nature, the vine, the Dionysus, as he was the soul of nature.

He was the gulls screaming at low tide and tearing the small crabs from among the knotted weeds.

People of Sparta

Hyacinths, whetted steel, barbarism, the intensity of mind and spirit of the people of Sparta rivalled the people of Athens itself.

Athens forever remains centre of the Greek world, suave, civilized, maker of finished warrior, statesman and poet, one whose greatest is said to have remembered with joy when dying that he had contributed to the glory of Athens (not the priceless treasure of his drama) but the fact that as a youth he had met in the Plataean grove a Persian who would not forget him. Athens is forever set in a ring of amethyst. Athens, like strange worlds scientists tell us of, seems to be lighted by another sun; dawn flows violet, at noon the rocks on Hymettus cast violet shade, at evening the whole is one flower; the jagged peaks of the mountains, not only in colour but in shape, are obvious violet-heads cut in stone and granite, a rock-wreath of purple flowers.

A suavity—a fragrance—Athens—moderation!

Laconia—Lacedaemonia!

Strange savage custom and superstition, the boys sacrificing outside the city, under the patronage of Apollo, young dogs to the god of war, as no other Greeks, and as no other Greeks turned into young animals to fight with fist and teeth, inflicting and receiving ungainly savage injuries. Yet not far from this level gymnasium, circled with its gaping ditch, is a temple of the Muses, "because the Lacedaemonians do not go out to battle to the sound of trumpet but to the music of flute and lyre and harp".

Strange contradiction, a people subtle, sensitive and yet most grossly savage, iron, brass, new process of welding armour and smelting ore for statue and temple floors, intense justice, Lycurgus, a name among the few law-makers of the world, Sparta, the law-making, the law-inventing, law-abiding, the dances of young women before the chaste and valiant Artemis, and the tearing of young men, gouging of eyes, searing of flesh in the name of holiest Apollo.

Perhaps (as today psychologists would tell us) the suppression that made for this strict observance of the law, virtue and beauty, needed by analogy a violent outburst. Cleomenes, the Spartan ruler, characterizes the spirit of his people. Daring in the world of the supernatural as in his worldly affairs and martial exploits, subtle in intellect, a giant in courage, he tampered with the Delphic oracle, bribed the priestess to predict disaster to his enemies, worked valiantly through the tangle he himself had made about him, and at last "died in a fit of madness".

It was in his reign that Xerxes led his army into Greece.

For one moment, for one second, for one heartbeat, the living organism of the world or the spirit of the world seemed in jeopardy, as if beyond this earth and the spirit or daemon of this earth, another was watching, questioning: shall this our earth be a creature of sensuous, high-strung, feminine, changeable, fluid character, given first to the lure of the senses, a creation of the sun but of an Eastern sun, myrrh mingled with spices, men beautiful, with the half-male, ringed and braceletted beauty, with hair braided below the shoulders falling in ringlets, odorous, with a golden crown inset with the image of an Eastern sun, or shall the West prevail?

Athens standing mid-way, given to intellectual subtlety and intellectual vagaries, with breadth, with desire to achieve, Athens reaching toward Asia with its chain of peerless islands. Athens begetter of poets and lover of poets from farthest island and foreign coast, daring colonizer of the Asian sea-board, Athens, a city set forever on a hill, valiant, undaunted, its personality expressed in every scratch and hollow of its paving-stones, and stamped on the heart of every citizen, as the owl and helmet on the coinage of its city, Athens, a light forever— the woman with the helmet or the male with the embroidered and purple sleeve?

Athens, it is true, is the goal of all our striving, the rock-island, beauty, moderation, the Muses waving violets! But beyond Athens, like the tears we cannot shed in hearing certain unwonted phrasing of music or the timbre of perfect rhythm, beyond the consciousness, beyond the intellect, is the terror of the unexpressed, the fear that rages, tearing us like the young men each other, inchoate, undefined, or the beauty expressed and dying to be worshipped dead, a beauty beyond the ecstasy that makes song, the spirit of the Hyacinthia, the Spartan festival. Beyond Athens' ivory and silver, standing supreme upon the Parthenon, is the Athene brass and iron and red roses, another, sacrificing even the mind, her lovely citadel for a region of blank terror and unexploited beauty.

Leonidas, a citizen of Sparta with three hundred men of Lacedaemonia, met the entire strength of Persia in a mountain pass below Thessaly.

Beyond reason, beyond the technical expression of dramatic poem or music or chiselling of statue, this action remains part of the realm of the sublimely inexpressible ... the hundred and their leader slain!

O passer-by, tell the Lacedaemonians that we die here obeying their orders.

It is significant that an outsider, a poet of Cos, affiliated with Athens, Simonides, should have crystallized the spirit of Sparta in this heroic epitaph. Laconia bred few poets. Its spirit was essentially the spirit of action, but action technically perfect, the war-dance, the dance of maidens, the marching to battle, the meeting and the slaying of the enemy, even the mode and manner of death were self-conscious, dramatic, trained, perfected actions, technical actions; a life lived as a poem is written, a death met as the hero in the Athenian drama meets it, with stately posture, with inevitable grace, with enviable reserve.

To write a poem, to carve a Hermes or Diadumenos requires a lifetime of absolute service, and many previous dedicated lives. Calamos, Scopas not only spent the ardour of their brain and spirit in perfecting their technique, but others had already attained, achieved, invented manner, method and mannerism of which they were no mean inheritors. The three hundred had inherited somewhat a technique of heroism; they achieved a perfection never yet attained, never to be surpassed, at Thermopylae.

But the spirit of Greece, though the various members of it are so singularly divergent, is one. Thessaly, Thermopylae, Thebes, Athens, Argos, Sparta are names we love and turn over in our hands like unset jewels, making new patterns or stringing them upon a chain to add and add like a child threading its beads, new names, new jewels, Thessaly, wild woods, wild beasts, branch of a tree, a moss-agate; Thermopylae, the quivering ruby, shot with fire; Thebes, rock and walls, a black Phoenician jade; Athens, obviously the crystal, reflecting the outer world yet intellectualizing all things to dream and vision; Argos, some curious buried moonstone; Sparta, great ruby, yet no flawless jewel with such inner fire as that perfect flame, Thermopylae. And on from Sparta, we have name on name of tiny city, fringing the sea. These names seem to me like a handful of tiny pearls, perhaps in the larger reading of history, valueless, but, with little fleck and flaw, full of colour and charm, a handful of seed-pearls, made to be strung about the throat of a small child.

There is Croceae with its stones "like river stones", which add to the "beauty of fish-pond and ornamental waters". There are the eighteen cities along the irregular points of the sea-coast, "all that remain of what were once the twenty-four cities of the Eleutherolancones". In one we find a "grove with fountains", in another a special little stretch of sand where the "sea shore has pebbles beautiful in shape and of all kinds of colours".

In one town, Atlanta paused, thirsty with hunting; in another is a mysterious little patch of fruitful ground called "Dionysus' garden". There is a fountain in one of these smaller cities where once the passer-by paused and beheld as in a mirror a vision to gladden his heart, of ships passing, strange ships with golden figure-heads and purple sails, where all care was forgotten; a picture to be remembered all a man's life, to ease his soul in dying. But alas—"the peculiarity of the water was stopped for all times by a woman washing her dirty linen in it".

Further on is a temple to Ino, sea-goddess, who like Thetis seems nearest to a child's ideal of a queen-protectress or sea-mother. There is another statue in a temple but we do not know its name for it is covered by a "quantity of garlands".

Again there is a Castor and Pollux, brothers of a fairy tale, standing in the open, "these the sea cannot move from their position though in winter-time it dashes violently over the rock". And further on is an Eros, playmate of children, in a grove.

There are the fifty impractical curious girls, daughters of the sea, and there is the small wood sacred to these Nereids, "for the story goes that they climbed up to this place to see Pyrrhus, the son of Achilles, when he went off to Sparta to marry Hermione".

There is our Athene again, this time called Cyparissia, who seems to join hands with the beautiful one, the flawless, sprung from the sea, cast with froth and iridescent spray upon Cythera, the island off the Laconian coast, pendant, as it were to the chain of tiny seed-pearls, giant pearl, shot through with violet and rose-tinted lights.

From Megara to Corinth

Pausanias tells us simply that in the statues of the Venerable Ones, the Erinyes, "there is nothing horrible". (It was Aeschylus, who imagined them with serpents in their hair.) None of the statues of the infernal deities, he says, suggests anything terrible or malignant. Poignant tribute to the sanity of the Athenian sculptor and the Athenian people who needed no shock of the bizarre or twisted Gothic monster to frighten them from evil and to drive them back to God.

The God in the infernal regions was as sane as the god in heaven or on earth. The serpent at her feet and the Nike, bird-creature, her own concentrated, vivid, winged and perfect self, resting upon her outstretched palm, are subject alike to the mind of Athene. The wisdom of the serpent (knowledge of sub-conscious regions and the supernatural) and inspiration (the bird-wisdom, flight, discernment of ecstasy and beauty) were nothing to her if they took from her, her poise and sanity.

There is nothing horrible in the statues of gods, half-gods, maidens and winged deities of the Acropolis, no disfigurement of brow or grotesque deformity of figure to shock humanity, to paralyze and subjugate the will. Even the Medusa, the Gorgon, Pausanias writes, on the "south wall which looks from the Acropolis to the theatre" appeals in line and moderation of expression, not to superstition and realms of hidden terror but to the intellect, and it is "wrought in gold".

"Celestial Aphrodite is the oldest of those that are called Fates", reads an inscription on the base of a statue of the goddess set in an Athenian garden. Aphrodite and Athene do not always stand victor and victim as at the gates of Troy.

So in passing on, along the road from Megara to Corinth, we need not lose the patronage of the Grey-eyed Athenian because we wander in gardens over-run with myrtle, dark with roses.

Yet the Isthmus is not all a garden. Stern, implacable strength, rulers of elements, spirits, rulers of the body deified, heroes stand equal to the queen of men and gods. Statues of athletes, victors in the Isthmian games, writes Pausanias, stand on one side of the temple of Poseidon and on the other, "pine-trees planted in a row, mostly in a straight line".

Mostly in a straight line; there is wind and rough sea, there is strength to greet us devotees of Nike, victors in the Isthmus games, young men, powerful in frame, with small heads (wrought by early sculptors in the half-archaic manner), with strong white feet, granite rock outstanding against the dark wall of the temple, brothers of Dioscuri, brothers to Perseus and Heracles, brothers to the mighty shaft of pine; serious of mien, sacred beings set apart forever for some strength of thigh or dexterity of wrist or swiftness of glance, for daring or fortitude, with intellect of brow shared equally, with intellect of hand and shaft of shoulder-blade and ankle and turn of knee, winners in the Isthmian games.

Later ages crowded this temple with tawdry statue, ornate Triton, dolphin and sea-horses. But I see it as of the earlier times, rough grass grown almost to the knee of some young winner of the pentathlon, or heroic figure, the symmetry of the conventional rendering of the close-fitting cap of fine carved curls, slightly worn by storm and wind, the taut hips and shoulders breaking shock of weather as the hero stands alert, bright against the great down-sweeping branch of the black pine.

"On the ascent to Acrocorinthos there is also a temple to Aphrodite." I cannot at the moment visualize this temple, not the many others sacred to the goddess, but rather, just across the border, in Argolis, near Mycenae, a small temple Pausanias beautifully describes for us, the shrine of another queen, august and beautiful, Hera of heaven.

A river flows above the temple, opposite the great crags of a gigantic mountain; the temple, small, compact, is set, vivid, brilliant semi-circle of marble beside the ravine into which the river flows. The mountains opposite the temple are sacred, the mountains near the temple and the "ground below the temple", each for some peculiar characteristic are equally revered; the ground, the earth is electric but with separate and distinctive powers, as the power of arms may differ from the passion of the knees or shoulders. But all surround this small queen, this white and flawless deity, as with one flame.

Upon the bank of the river, a flower grows. What flower? Pausanias names it asterion. We read elsewhere that the honeysuckle was beloved of Hera. Is this the tense and wax-like fragrant flower, clambering across rough log and bramble and low bushes, the young women took to Hera, plaiting her crowns of leaves and pointed blossoms?

The sun falls upon this temple, but the pillars do not dazzle; they are a soft delicate carving of some precious marble, stained perhaps a soft fawn-yellow like the yellow of the honey-flower; quarried from special mountain to merge, mellow (not too intense and star-like) against the massive hillside.

There are statues in the precinct and within the temple, but we see rather heroes and gods themselves, men and living women; Orestes, seated, his hands clasped about his knees, thoughtful, somehow human, at peace, not the tragic Orestes, with haunted eyes, we meet before the Parthenon.

Of the statues of Hera, the oldest and most sacred was made of a mild pear-tree. Strange fragrance of the tree wafted through arch and portico, billow upon billow of the fragrant fruit-branch, strength of the ripe wood rooted in the earth, women, priestesses, moving with friendly dignity, robes falling from firm breasts and slender hips, men, quiet in the porches—Orestes, at peace.

The old temple, the flawless jewel was burnt. Chryseis, the young priestess, fell asleep and the flame of her lamp up-darting in a sudden rising of storm-wind across the mountain, caught at the fringe binding the curtain, strung between two pillars. The heavy fringe swept her forehead but Chryseis did not move. Pungent odours of the treasured hidden spices, fragrant spice and scorching woodwork and small wooden carving lapped and rent across with fire, until it was too late.

Chryseis fled from the shelter of the precinct (from her mother, her protectress) fearing the rage of a people who had trusted her with the most sacred relics of their country. She turned in her peril to the Alean Athene. We do not know what comfort the goddess gave her, only this: "Athough such a misfortune had befallen them, the Argives did not remove the statue of Chryseis, but it is there to this day in front of the burnt temple."

The burnt temple—this is one among others touched on, in these few pages. This book on Corinth is crowded with name of king and hero and maiden! Each sets up in the mind a long train of imaginative scenes and reconstructed pictures. The book on Corinth contains as well legend and tale of Argolis (this land sacred to Hera), of Troezen, so closely allied through history and legend to Athens, of Phaedra and the special myrtle with leaves frayed at the edge; the leaves always grew torn and broken after the day when Phaedra, standing in the garden of the palace, finally realized her hopelessness. The queen of Theseus gazed with dignity, with serene eyelids, past her waiting-woman, past the fig-trees and the other myrtle-tangles and pomegranates, but she saw nothing of the garden or far hill or blue outstretching bay. Her mind recorded not even the feel of the rough branch and threads of the leafed fibre which stained her aching fingers "as she wreaked her agony on the leaves of myrtle".

We read of plane-trees, of fields fitted for the growth of olives, of the wild olive, the special fruited olive and the olive suitable for rearing within gardens; of peculiar hyacinth, worn by the boys in the winter procession, "in colour and size" resembling the ordinary hyacinth, yet differing subtly in some detail of stem or leaf or spacing of flower-cluster.

We hear of dreams, of Pan called deliverer for he helped the people of the country when plague threatened them, "he showed dreams". Sleep and the Muses received sacrifice for "sleep is a god most friendly to the Muses". Some peculiar characteristics of sunlight, of dawn, of dusk, of the night darkness must have acted on the intense and vivid imagination of this people, bordering Corinth, close allied to Athens, for again we hear of a dream "sent from Athene", of "sleep and dream" and "sleep the bountiful" worshipped in the most sacred precincts of a temple.

One vivid detail haunts me, as I pass too, too swiftly with undue lack of ceremony and scant worship, the many temples, the shrines and statues crowding the worn road-way. Many gardens tempt me but I do not enter. I am a pilgrim, worn, travel-stained, fervid yet not ready to enter the porches of the holiest Aphrodite. Many fragrant branches of wild azalea and wild rose-tree brush dusty hair and strained eyelids. No voice of syren tempts us but a stronger voice, the voice of the real lover who cannot pause to kiss eyelid or wave of hair or subtle line of throat or ankle, loving it all so much, loving the spirit set within the body no less and no more than the body sheltering the spirit. Is not all Corinth the body Aphrodite, all Greece, the beauty of Athene? Where can we pause, how to differentiate?

In Hellas, generalization finds expression in the particular. In individuals of her people is the answer to her abstract questions. The qualities of her spirit live in the names of her poets.

This one is little known, though with Anyte, Sappho and Erinna she rivalled the greatest singers of her day and of all history. Her poems are lost. Yet this Telesilla was "otherwise remarkable among women".

Flame, steel, flash of sword, walls broken and walls fallen, no mythical Penthesilea sent against godlike Achilles—but a girl, a woman, a reality.

Disaster untold upon the Argives, the sacrifice of those within the forest who finding no quarter granted (though appealing to an enemy from a sacred precinct) chose a swift expedient and set "themselves and the grove on fire together".

Then in an Argos "stript of men", the valour of Athene entered the body of a woman; Telesilla "manned the walls". She cried to the slaves, the young boys, the girls, her comrades in the games, the young women whom she loved and their mothers, to defy Lacedaemonia and the men of Sparta.

Beyond the theatre, in front of the temple of Aphrodite, was later placed a statue, Telesilla; at her feet, the scrolls of her love-poetry, in her hand, a helmet.

A Poet in the Wilderness: Songs of Anacreon

When we have found our own world (when behind us in the clearing of great pine woods, we know perfectly and forever that the wild legions of Pan track, unmolested, the wild deer and mountain-panther; where the hill-trail winds to the sun and beyond it a canyon heaps rock on rock to meet another hill, and the ground-squirrel and the snake wreak tireless vengeance on each other's delicate offspring), we would be disappointed if we found an altar or a broken pillar or some other tribute of man to prove that he had trapped a spirit. Here the gods are perfectly nonchalant. We see as the tide moves under the surface of the sea the huge indifferent shrug of giant shoulders.

They shrug their shoulders at Europe. They invent new, strange and godless gestures. I know their impertinence. I too know something of their uncouth arid grace.

But they shall not forget. The past is about them and it shall be their future. They must be prodded out of their comfortable nonchalance, out of the pine-woods, out of the sea, out of the flutter of bird-wings and the padding of the panther, back into the hearts of men.

How shall we prod them out? I, for one, would do it by gest for gest, nonchalance for nonchalance, indifference for indifference. I draw a strip of curtain across the too insistent greatness of the world without, the mountain and its peak on peak of green that drops with all its dramatic, forceful, barbaric grandeur, sheer into a jagged hill of granite; granite, out into fine, perpendicular lines of irregular pointed lights and rare intermediate shadow which again drops straight into the sea itself; to flat surface of rock in one bay, in another, perfect sand-shelf and waves always changing, always clear and lucid, small and great mingling, wedded here as if at the heart of a great whirlpool, east and tumultuous west at last, static and at peace.

I draw the curtain across my window, across them, their impertinence and their greatness. I cannot bear to think of them. But with my fingers stained with moss and scratched with whortleberry and oak-tangle, I open a little Tauchnitz volume.

With my fingers too, rather than with my eyes, I read these poems.

Ionic volutes—delicate and ringed—white shells with the inner side of pearl—indented cup with the chiselling as fine as the pattern of the under-leaf lining of the wine itself—firm bone and fibre—framework of the wing of a dove—intricate, puzzling yet precise curves wrought upon a lyre-frame—all this—more and much more—and to concentrate my senses, struggling now with faint, exotic perfumes, pungent and stimulating, not quite familiar, with colours, rose and the violet of the rainbow, I close my eyes and with my fingers like one blind would find my way about this poetry.

I am not fleeing for sanctuary across the dead lintels of the past, into an unearthed temple, old lava-broken porches and courtyards, swept clean of scattered ashes, petrified corn grains, stone apple-cores and cinders.

I am fleeing from the present, pursued by present-day

art-theorists, serpent-crowned Erinyes. I think myself rather beyond the fashion, ultra-modern. I feel when I read a fragment of a melic poet as I felt when I stood on the steps of the Athenian propylaea. I had strayed then into a temple-porch about to be built. I looked for cranes and engines, for the lifting of the heavy stones. Those columns, in the Greek sun, were so very new and many of them splintered exactly as if cut with machines for some definite constructive purpose.

There was no one about. No group of tourists or visitors such as one used to meet in Rome; Rome, as I saw it years ago, was vast and complete and dead. The columns splintering the crystal light of the Acropolis were in the process of being built, small perfect things!

So with these poems of Anacreon. They are quite new. I am certain they are waiting to be read. No one has read them, no one has touched these pages. They are new things, about to be found—new goblets, new lyre-frames, new carved Ionic capitals, new bowls for un-plucked roses, new sandal-clasps, new shoulder-buckles, new yet not new—worn once and put away as the over-sophisticated traveller hides away the garments he returns to, after many years' seclusion in the wilderness, mark of caste and distinction.

Will they return, these gods (over-sophisticated travellers), if they find their old drinking-goblets, their old trinkets are of real value, give pleasure to real people? Will they, if we burn with the ecstasy of new spiritual possessions, turn, as a child may turn, when we no longer wish it to, clutching at its possession, its own possession cast off by it, but re-desired and passionately desired when we possess it utterly.

I do not know. But I feel genuinely indifferent to their vast shrugs, their prodigal aloofness. In reality, I give back shrug for shrug. My thoughts are with a poet!

Anacreon is one of the poets selected for Meleager's garland, his is the dedicatory poem, prefacing the Anthology. Meleager, the poet-critic, who matches flower and poet, as a lover finding suitable offering for many, though singularly diverse and never wearying mistresses, chooses for Anacreon the honeysuckle. So much has the most poignant critic and poet and poet-lover offered him. For history, we know that he was born in a small town on the coast of Asia Minor, was driven out by the inroads of the Persians, lived as an aristocrat at the court of an island-ruler, at Sámos, again mingled with the chosen spirits of his generation at Athens, and returning late in life, died in his native city.

Yet the poet is gone. Though we might wish to touch his hand, to make his humanity as important as his divinity, it is not possible.

I should like to have touched his hand, to have counted his imperfections, to have said (to lure him to some outbreak of fine, poetic fervour), "Yes, all that, poetry is not enough—humanity is the thing that matters—as below, so are the gods above, let us get down, underneath things—learn, in humility, true greatness." Ah—but he would not let me!

He is gone. There floats this legend through old text-books, a date, an anecdote, but he, he himself is gone. He is gone, cruel in his immortality. He has left us—he has left *me*, and before me fingering this little volume, there is a path, set with small white paving-stones, a little edge of white marble, laid in long, even, slender, grace-ful blocks, stone blocks, imperceptible curves, two steps, columns, very small, very perfect.

Across a bay of blue unbroken water, there is a sound of flutes, delicate rhythms and with a background of more fragile notes, but distinct too, of perfect, simple measure, easy to follow, easy to find!

His Ionic columns, set against near, dark blue of early evening-sky, are a gate, a shelter from undefined yet ever imminent peril from outside, a doorway to a garden.

For the spring has come, that is what his words say; curling our hands about the cup of one of his rose-blooms we see, or *feel* further, further than the perfection of his carvings, carvings made to endure, but, like all static beauty, poignant in the hearts of those who over-love it.

Spring has come. See how the crane flies, how the duck has made his journey. See the baby (we call him Eros) under the great white rose-tree. An enormous bee has pricked his finger—stupid, silly, adorable surprise—ah—she who stoops to soothe him—the curve of the white back—and the white rose leaves, brushing the soft shoulder!

Ionic capitals, washed in honey and white rain—gold and marble and honey and tints of yellow-grapes.

Always that baby whom we call Eros—always the roses—red and yellow, and tints of cream and tea-rose colour—and a swallow who breaks from a low dwarf-laurel bush (just now in the rosebud-stage of flower) with almost too insistently shrill a song to match the far, simple murmuring of the lyre-string.

Too blue a swallow with too sweet a note!

"Let joy not be intense," says Eros, though he knows not what he means. "Spring has come," says Eros again, but a spring, so tender, so gentle, so gradual, insinuated with such delicate subtlety that it can never go.

This poet is the tenderest of lovers!

There is no strife—no wavering—no gauche or awkward gesture—only in our ears, this one low, insistent, ceaseless rhythm—in our hands, rose leaves—in our minds, the vision of that lovely goddess and of her sulky baby.

Above all, there is no searching after the great majestic beings who, philosophers have said, govern the universe. She, whom we saw, was no goddess, in that sense, neither was she a woman; a flower she was and is! Let the great keep their hilltops.

Curled Thyme

Where the Greek voice speaks there are rocks. But these Sicilian rocks of Theocritus, particularly of the twentieth Bucolic with which I specifically deal, are sunk a layer beneath rich soil. Theocritean rocks are covered with earth, rich loam and successive sun-baked, sun-broken and un-crumbled layers of oak leaves, blades of rank grass and reeds and many feathery, dusty, dried and broken herbs and flowers, witches' herbs and vine leaves and withered berries of grapes. Only by study of this surface, ripe, rich, decadent only in the sense in which a brittle sun-baked July leaf is decadent, do we realize the real quality of those rocks … Greek even if once-removed, Sicilian. In Theocritus are layers of rocks, and under the rocks is fire, ever ready to break out volcanic, infernal one might say, were there for the Greek any inferno but that of suppression and inhibition and actual bodily death.

This is the world of Theocritus, as different from that of Euripides as black earth from limpid water, water surface that reflects images of Olympians, pure spirits, as if the sun threw colour and fire, different yet the same, passing through that Athenian intellect. For at Athens there is light and one has never seen such light, not in dream, not in vision, not light reflected from rock-pools, nor light from the ridges of mountains. There is gold in Egypt, there is air doubtless, warmed and coloured and steeped in gold in Assyria, in Phoenicia, in Libya, gold beneath and above, there is heat in Assyria; there is colour everywhere, there is *light* in one city.

But there is shadow elsewhere. There are spaces of blackness, warm and soft and restful; blackness which spreads soft cushions where we may rest, blackness of dream, witchcraft, blackness too of rest, of mirth, blackness as of a great curtain against which the figures of Theocritus stand, brilliant images, red and rust-colour, black-purple, mops of tangled hair, goat-herd, goat and kid and bull, and divine images, drawn with the richness of a Rubens, designed not to draw us toward the sky and its enchantments but to bring us close to wholesome, passionate things of earth.

She hates me and I sweat with agony "as a rose with dew" says the boy.

We have often met this boy. We have known him throughout the whole of Hellenic literature. We had grown weary of his fifth-century perfections; we had grown tired of him, friend and companion of the great, pupil, essence of the divine, drawing his master to contemplation, through repression, of the abstract and geometrical. We had seen him, tall and serene, amid the banqueters of the early dramatist, Plato, man of the world, Athenian and poet. We had worshipped him, "the morning star among the living", but all stars, all suns, must set. So we followed him again, half furtively into the hidden gardens of effete, outlying suburbs; followed him and again, loved him half furtively. Till we grew sick of the roses and the myrrh and turned with relief to the late epigrammatists who made of him a mark for poignant satire.

Satire, the death-blow, resounding of hammer-strokes on already broken bones, virulent acid to eat away decay, has too its death-blow, meets in the end defeat. For when the body is purged or slain or dead, there is a new body, whether of individuals, of nations, of modes of thought, of literatures, or feelings, or emotions. Beyond life there is death, beyond exuberance, there is inevitable decay. Equally beyond death, there is life, old forms in new environments.

Through the medium of this boy, a traditional figure for inspiration and for mirth, Theocritus, for the first time, weds beauty with the jeer at beauty. The Greek country boy loves Eunica. He has found her in the city. He has never before seen rose and pink so divinely mingled on so white a face. With a tittering sneer of Eunica at "dank lips, black hands, rank smell", by a subtle, inner reading of the poet, we sniff not so much the grosser sweepings of the ox-stalls as fresh hay and new-turned loam.

Rather it is from the girl Eunica we turn. Not because of the boy's crude tirade at her, not because he tells us, "she spit at him, mouthed and played the whore" but because we ourselves see her with our own eyes, standing on that squalid pavement (the Alexandria of Theocritus' later period), her pleated shawl dust-stained and hinting of dead myrrh, the tattered fringe of her under-vest grey and lustreless in the noon-day sunlight, her yellow-tinted curls showing the marks of a too ambitious iron beside the boy's clustering locks, burnt crisp with Sicilian sun.

Beauty and the jeer at beauty meet. Look, he says, am I not a man? My hair curls like the selena-flower, my eyebrows are lustrous black, and such and such and such fine phrases he uses, parsley, honeycomb, inept and futile embellish the description of his own charms.

The poet jeers at beauty, destroying with one hand, re-welding with the other. We hear him play two themes upon a double-pipe. The girls may jilt me, says the boy, and he becomes a figure of satire comparing his stupid eyes to the beauty of the Athenian goddess, but his music he says is sweet and we know that this is true.

At the end of this idyll, the poet lets the boy play for us soft, yet full and ripe music, under great wind-swept pine-trees, a tone lower, no shrill Dionysic ecstatic flute-note, but reeds, rich and quiet.

Here the names we have met and worshipped in distant stars, again worshipped in temples and loved on earth, and loved over-familiarly and grown to tire of, are renewed for us beyond their death, a renewal, a new life. For Kypris, white star, met Adonis in the shadow of great oak-woods and clinging to the rough trunk of an oak-tree wept for him there, and the Moon herself, white slaying scimitar, stood, only a Lady, after all, tired, with disillusioned feet, upon a hill in Latmos.

Born Hilda Doolittle, H.D. (1886–1961) was an American poet and novelist associated with Imagism, an avant-garde literary movement that emerged in London during the early twentieth century. Her first and perhaps best-known collection of poetry, *Sea Garden* (1916), exemplifies the precise imagery and sharp language favored by Imagism and her contemporaries Ezra Pound and William Carlos Williams. H.D.'s writing was often deeply personal, merging her unstable private life, marred as it was by frequent illness and loss, with the evocative images and stories of the ancient world. Together with her companion Bryher, she traveled throughout Europe, in particular to Greece, and to Egypt, sites that would continue to inspire her late into her life and have a profound impact on her final poems, such as the revisionary epic *Helen in Egypt* (1961). Though somewhat overshadowed by her male contemporaries in historical and critical accounts of modernist movements, H.D. is one of the most important and inimitable writers of her time.

MICHAEL GREEN is a Wolfson Scholar and PhD candidate in the Department of History of Art at University College London. He works within the intersections of art, literature, and psychoanalysis, and his current research engages with how H.D.'s writings have been used in contemporary art practices from the 1970s to the present.

THE *EKPHRASIS* SERIES

"Ekphrasis" is traditionally defined as the literary representation of a work of visual art. One of the oldest forms of writing, it originated in ancient Greece, where it referred to the practice and skill of presenting artworks through vivid, highly detailed accounts. Today, "ekphrasis" is more openly interpreted as one art form, whether it be writing, visual art, music, or film, that is used to define and describe another art form, in order to bring to an audience the experiential and visceral impact of the subject.

The *ekphrasis* series from David Zwirner Books is dedicated to publishing rare, out-of-print, and newly commissioned texts as accessible paperback volumes. It is part of David Zwirner Books's ongoing effort to publish new and surprising pieces of writing on visual culture.

OTHER TITLES IN THE *EKPHRASIS* SERIES

On Contemporary Art
César Aira

Ramblings of a Wannabe Painter
Paul Gauguin

Thrust
Michael Glover

Pissing Figures 1280–2014
Jean-Claude Lebensztejn

The Psychology of an Art Writer
Vernon Lee

Degas and His Model
Alice Michel

28 Paradises
Patrick Modiano and Dominique Zehrfuss

Summoning Pearl Harbor
Alexander Nemerov

Chardin and Rembrandt
Marcel Proust

Letters to a Young Painter
Rainer Maria Rilke

Giotto and His Works in Padua
John Ruskin

Duchamp's Last Day
Donald Shambroom

FORTHCOMING IN 2020

A Balthus Notebook
Guy Davenport

Two Cities
Cynthia Zarin

Visions and Ecstasies
Selected Essays
H.D.

Published by
David Zwirner Books
529 West 20th Street, 2nd Floor
New York, New York 10011
+ 1 212 727 2070
davidzwirnerbooks.com

Managing Director: Doro Globus
Editorial Director: Lucas Zwirner

Editor: Michael Green
Project Manager: Elizabeth Gordon
Proofreader: Dorothy Feaver

Design: Michael Dyer / Remake
Production Manager: Jules Thomson
Production Assistant:
Elizabeth Koehler
Printing: VeronaLibri, Verona

Typeface: Arnhem
Paper: Holmen Book Cream,
80 gsm

Publication © 2019
David Zwirner Books

Introduction © 2019
Michael Green

Distributed in the United States
and Canada by
Simon & Schuster, Inc.
1230 Avenue of the Americas
New York, New York 10020
simonandschuster.com

Distributed outside the
United States and Canada by
Thames & Hudson, Ltd.
181A High Holborn
London WC1V 7QX
thamesandhudson.com

ISBN 978-1-64423-023-7

Library of Congress
Control Number: 2019911561